JEAN AN[OUILH]

Thieves Carnival

A PLAY IN FOUR ACTS

Translated by Lucienne Hill

SAMUEL FRENCH, INC.

45 WEST 25TH STREET   NEW YORK 10010

7623 SUNSET BOULEVARD   HOLLYWOOD 90046

LONDON   *TORONTO*

THIEVES' CARNIVAL

STORY OF THE PLAY

This most successful of Anouilh's works in the United States is an excellent lark, loaded with humorous whims, romance and masquerades. The scene is set in a palatial home where two attractive young girls reside. The home is invaded by three affectionate thieves on the one hand, and by a country bumpkin on the other. A lovely romance blooms instantly between one of the girls and the youngest thief. Being a very honest fellow, he cannot in conscience accept her love, and instead turns with vengeance toward his job. But she is swifter in her wiles than he is in his⟍

Sound Effects Record or tape $22.50, plus $3.00 for postage and handling.

THIEVES' CARNIVAL

CHARACTERS

PETERBONO ⎫
HECTOR ⎬ *Thieves*
GUSTAVE ⎭
LORD EDGARD
LADY HURF
JULIETTE ⎫ *her nieces*
EVA ⎭
DUPONT-DUFORT SENIOR
DUPONT-DUFORT JUNIOR
THE TOWN CRIER
THE POLICEMAN
THE NURSEMAID
THE LITTLE GIRL
THE MUSICIAN

4

Thieves' Carnival

ACT ONE

*The public gardens of a watering-place which saw its
heyday in the 1880's. In the middle, a bandstand.
The orchestra is represented by a single MUSICIAN,
who at the rise of the Curtain is executing a solo of
superlative virtuosity on the clarinet. A woman deck-
chair ATTENDANT goes to and fro. Summer VISITORS
stroll up and down to the rhythm of the music. In
the foreground EVA and HECTOR are locked in a
dramatic screen embrace. The MUSIC stops. So does
the kiss, from which HECTOR emerges, reeling a little.
Applause for the MUSICIAN.*

HECTOR. *(Covered in confusion.)* I say, steady. They're
applauding us!

EVA. *(Bursts out laughing.)* Of course not, it's the
orchestra. I must say you appeal to me enormously.

HECTOR. *(Instinctively fingering his hair and moustache)* What do you like about me, specially?

EVA. Everything. *(She blows him a kiss.)* We mustn't
stay here, it's too risky. I'll see you tonight at eight in
the Phoenix bar. And if you should meet me with my
aunt, whatever you do, pretend you don't know me.

HECTOR. *(Yearningly.)* Your little hand, once more.

EVA. Careful. My aunt's old friend Edgard is over there
by the bandstand reading his paper. He'll see us. *(She
holds out her hand, but turns away to watch LORD
EDGARD.)*

HECTOR. *(Passionately.)* I want to inhale the perfume
of your hand!

*(He bends over her hand, and surreptitiously draws a
jeweler's eyeglass from his pocket to take a closer
look at EVA's rings. EVA withdraws her hand, unaware of the manœuvre.)*

5

EVA. Till tonight. *(She goes.)*

HECTOR. *(Weak at the knees.)* My beloved— *(He follows her out of sight, then comes down stage again, putting away his eyeglass, and mutters with icy self-possession.)* A good two hundred thousand. And not a flaw in the lot.

(At this point the TOWN CRIER *enters with his drum and the crowd gather round to listen.)*

TOWN CRIER. Townsmen of Vichy! The Municipality, anxious to preserve the well-being and security of the invalids and bathers, issues a warning for their information and protection! Numerous complaints from visitors have been lodged at the Town Hall and at the main police station, Market Street. A dangerous pack of pickle-pockets—

(He has a little trouble with this word, at which the CLARINET plays a little accompaniment. The TOWN CRIER swings round on him, furious.)

—a dangerous pack of pockpickets—

(Again the CLARINET renders the word in music.)

—is at this very hour within our gates. The local police is on the watch. Members of the Force, in plain clothes and in uniform, are ready to protect our visitors—

(Indeed, even as he speaks POLICEMEN are threading their several ways gracefully through the CROWD.)

Visitors are nevertheless requested to exercise the greatest possible caution, particularly on the highway, in public parks and in all other places of public resort. A reward in kind is offered by the Tourist Association to anyone supplying information leading to the apprehension of the felons! Tell your friends!

(A roll of DRUMS. During the proclamation HECTOR has relieved the TOWN CRIER of his enormous copper watch and bulging purse. The CROWD scatters, and the DRUM and the HARANGUE are heard again further off. HECTOR takes a seat, and the CHAIR-WOMAN approaches.)

CHAIRWOMAN. Will you take a ticket, sir, please?

HECTOR. *(Largely.)* Since it's customary—
CHAIRWOMAN. That'll be five francs, please.

(While HECTOR feels for the money, the WOMAN steals his wallet, then the huge watch and the purse he has just taken from the TOWN CRIER.)

HECTOR. *(Seizing the hand on its next trip into his pocket)* Hey! What do you think you're up to?
(The WOMAN struggles to free herself, and loses her wig.)
Have you gone crazy? *(He lifts his own wig and moustache a trifle.)* It's me!

(The CHAIR ATTENDANT readjusts her wig. It is PETER-BONO.)

PETERBONO. Sorry, old chap. It's me too. Had a good day?
HECTOR. The purse and a watch, and a cigarette lighter.
PETERBONO. *(Examining them)* I know that watch. It's the Town Crier's and it's made of copper. I put it back into his pocket, the poor devil, that and the purse, which you'll find if you check up contains just fifteen cents and the receipt for a registered parcel. As for the lighter, we've already got nine hundred and three, out of which only a couple work. I've known you do better, my lad!
HECTOR. I've a date tonight with a girl who'll be mine before you can say mischief, and who wears over two hundred thousand francs worth of diamonds on her middle finger.
PETERBONO. We'll look into it. Have you noticed that little thing over there? The necklace?
HECTOR. *(Examining the girl through the fieldglasses he wears round his neck)* Phew! The stones are enormous!
PETERBONO. No wishful thinking. They're smaller to the naked eye. Still, off we go. Small change manœuvre. I get offensive and you interfere.
(They cross to the GIRL with a terrible affectation of indifference.)
Ticket? Ticket?

(The GIRL gives him a coin.)

(PETERBONO *begins to yell.*)

I've got no change! I tell you I've got no change! No change, do you hear? No change at all, I keep on telling you!

RECTOR. What's this? No change, eh? Excuse me, Mademoiselle, allow me to put this insolent baggage in her place!

(There follows a tussle under cover of which HECTOR investigates the clasp of the girl's necklace.)

THE GIRL. *(Violently freeing herself)* No, you don't!

HECTOR. *(Taken aback.)* What do you mean, no you don't!

PETERBONO. No you don't what?

THE GIRL. *(Lifting her wig. It is GUSTAVE.)* It's me.

HECTOR. *(Falling into a chair)* Charming!

PETERBONO. *(Exploding)* That's what comes of not working to plan! I can't rely on anybody! Running errands, that's all you're fit for! Errand boys! If it weren't for your poor old mother who put you in my charge to learn the business, you'd be out on your ear, the pair of you. Do you hear me? Out on your ear! And without your week's pay in lieu of notice, make no mistake! And complain to the union if you dare! I'll tell them a thing or two, the dance you've led me, both of you! *(To GUSTAVE.)* You! You haven't done a stroke today, naturally!

GUSTAVE. Yes I have. I've done two. First, there's this magnificent wallet.

PETERBONO. Let's have a look. *(He examines it, then searches himself anxiously.)* Where did you get this? Who from?

GUSTAVE. I got it in the Boulevard Ravachol off an old gentleman with a long white beard—

PETERBONO. *(Terrible in his anger.)* —check trousers, olive-green jacket and deer-stalker cap, am I right, pigeon-brain?

GUSTAVE. *(Quaking)* Yes, sir. Did you see me?

PETERBONO. *(Sinks into a chair, flattened by this latest*

blow.) That was me, idiot, that was me! At this rate we'll be lucky if we cover our expenses!

GUSTAVE. But I've got something else, Mr. Peterbono, sir.

PETERBONO. *(Profoundly discouraged.)* If it's something else you stole from me you can imagine my curiosity.

GUSTAVE. It isn't a thing, it's a girl. And she looks rich.

HECTOR. *(Jumping up)* Good God! Don't say it's the same girl. A redhead? About twenty-five? Name of Eva?

GUSTAVE. No. Dark hair, about twenty. Name of Juliet.

HECTOR. Oh, that's all right.

PETERBONO. What did you get?

GUSTAVE. Nothing yet. But I helped her fish a kid out of the Thermes Fountain. We sat in the sun to dry and we got talking. She told me she liked me.

PETERBONO. Any jewels?

GUSTAVE. One very fine pearl.

PETERBONO. Good. We must look into that. Hector, can you spare a moment this afternoon? other engagements permitting?

GUSTAVE. No! I'd like to handle this myself.

PETERBONO. What's this? What's this? Handle it yourself, would you? Well, whatever next?

GUSTAVE. It was me she took a fancy to.

PETERBONO. All the more reason. Hector will swallow her in one.

GUSTAVE. No, I tell you! Not this one!

PETERBONO. *(Severely.)* Gustave, listen to me. Your mother put you in my care, and I took you into the firm as assistant decoy. You're young and you're ambitious. That's fine. I was ambitious myself when I was your age. But just a minute! In our profession, as in all professions, you have to work your way up from the bottom. Hector here is the finest professional seducer I know this side of Monte Carlo. There's a chap who hits the bull's eye three times out of four, and take it from me, that's a pretty handsome average. You don't mean to tell me that you, a mere apprentice, expect to turn out better work than that?

GUSTAVE. To hell with it! I'll get her for myself.

PETERBONO. *(Tight-lipped.)* If you wish to do a job on the side in your spare time there's nothing to stop you. You'll owe me just the sixty-five per cent on what you make, that's all.

HECTOR. *(Who has been watching a* NURSEMAID *during this altercation)* Peter?

PETERBONO. Hector?

HECTOR. That nursemaid over there. See the gold chain?

PETERBONO. *(Contemptuously.)* Pooh! It's probably gilded fuse wire.

HECTOR. Listen, it's ten to seven. We've ten minutes in hand before supper.

PETERBONO. Very well, if you're set on it. We'll give her the "Three Musketeers" Manœuvre.

HECTOR. Three Musketeers Manœuvre?

PETERBONO. It's the classic routine for nursemaids. Number one gets off with her, number two plays ten little pigs with the baby, and number three starts whistling bugle-calls without a break to make her senses reel.

(They go. Enter LADY HURF *and* JULIETTE.)

pick up newspaper

JULIETTE. The little boy was barely five years old. He was only in up to his waist, but he was frightened and he kept falling over. He would have drowned, I'm sure.

LADY HURF. How dreadful! Have you noticed all these little chimney-pot hats everywhere? How absurd they look!

JULIETTE. Fortunately this young man came to the rescue. He was wonderful, and very sweet..

LADY HURF. All children are sweet at five. But at twelve they begin to get silly. That's why I never wanted any.

JULIETTE. I was talking about the young man, Aunt.

LADY HURF. Oh yes, of course. There's another of

those grotesque little hats. The young man was very sweet—yes, go on.

JULIETTE. That's all.

LADY HURF. We must invite him to dinner.

JULIETTE. He's gone. I'd never seen him before.

LADY HURF. Good. One always knows far too many people. Besides, I can't stand stories about drowning. Your poor uncle swam like a lump of lead. He drowned himself seven times, I could have hit him. Ah, there's Edgard. Edgard, have you seen Eva?

LORD EDGARD. (Appearing from behind his paper) How are you, my dear?

LADY HURF. I asked if you'd seen Eva.

LORD EDGARD. Eva? No, I haven't. That's very odd. Now what can I have done with her? Perhaps she's at the Baths.

LADY HURF. At seven o'clock at night? Don't be silly.

JULIETTE. Shall we try the Poenix bar? She often goes there.

LADY HURF. Edgard, don't stir from this spot for any reason whatsoever.

LORD EDGARD. Very good, my dear.

LADY HURF. (Going) But of course if you see her, run after her.

LORD EDGARD. Very good, my dear.

LADY HURF. Or better still, don't; you'd only lose her —just come and tell us which way she went.

LORD EDGARD. Very good, my dear.

LADY HURF. On second thoughts, no. You'd never manage to find us. Send one attendant after her, another attendant to let us know, and put a third in your place to tell us where you've gone so we can pick you up on the way home if we should happen to be passing.

LORD EDGARD. Very good, my dear.

(He retires, stunned, behind his paper. Exit LADY HURF with JULIETTE. Enter the DUPONT-DUFORTS, father and son, accompanied by the little jig on the clarinet, which is their signature tune.)

D.D. SENIOR. Let's follow. We'll meet them casually on the promenade, and try to tempt them to a cocktail. Didier, I don't know what's come over you. You, a hard-working, conscientious lad, brimful of initiative, and look at you. You're not paying an atom of attention to young Juliette.

D.D. JUNIOR. She snubs me.

D.D. SENIOR. What does that matter? To begin with, you aren't just anybody. You are Dupont-Dufort junior. Her aunt thinks a great deal of you. She's prepared to make any investment on your recommendation.

D.D. JUNIOR. That ought to be enough for us.

D.D. SENIOR. Son, in matters of money there's no such thing as enough. I'd far and away prefer you to pull off this marriage. Nothing short of that will put our bank fairly and squarely on its feet again. So let me see a bit of charm, a little fascination.

D.D. JUNIOR. Yes, Dad.

D.D. SENIOR. We couldn't wish for more propitious circumstances. They're bored to tears, and there's nobody here in the least presentable. So let's make ourselves agreeable, superlatively agreeable.

D.D. JUNIOR. Yes, Dad.

(Exeunt the DUPONT-DUFORTS. LORD EDGARD, *who has heard every word, looks over his "Times" to watch them go.* PETERBONO, HECTOR *and* GUSTAVE *come in dressed as soldiers as the* MUSICIAN *begins his second number. The* POLICEMEN *enter at the same time from the other side. They all perform a flirtatious little ballet round the* NURSEMAID, *the manœuvres of the* POLICEMEN *seriously impeding those of the* THREE THIEVES. *The* NURSEMAID *finally goes; the* POLICE-MEN, *twirling their white batons behind their backs, make gallant attempts to hinder her departure. During the ballet* LADY HURF *returns alone and goes to sit geside* LORD EDGARD. *The MUSIC stops at the exit of the* POLICEMEN *and the* NURSEMAID.)*

PETERBONO. *(Thwarted.)* Lads, that's the first time

I've ever known the Three Musketeers Manœuvre to miscarry.

LADY HURF. (*To* LORD EDGARD.) Well, Edgard my dear, and what have you done with yourself today?

LORD EDGARD. (*Surprised and embarrassed as always at* LADY HURF's *customary abruptness.*) I—er—I read the *Times*.

LADY HURF. (*Sternly.*) The same as yesterday?

LORD EDGARD. (*Ingenuously.*) Not the same copy as yesterday.

HECTOR. (*Who has been watching the scene, gives a whistle of admiration.*) See those pearls?

PETERBONO. Four millions!

HECTOR. How about it? What's it to be? Russian princes?

PETERBONO. No. She knows her onions by the look of her. Ruined Spanish noblemen.

GUSTAVE. That's bright of you. Whenever you masquerade as Spaniards you're rigged out like a couple of rats.

PETERBONO. Quiet, shaver! You're speaking of a trade you know nothing about.

GUSTAVE. Well, anyway, if you think I'm dressing up as your ecclesiastical secretary like the last time, it's no go. I'm not wearing a cassock in this heat.

PETERBONO. Gustave, you're trying my patience! Come along, home! Hector and I will be Spanish Grandees, and you'll put on that cassock, heat or no heat.

(*The unwilling* GUSTAVE *is borne away, to the accompaniment of a little jig on the clarinet.*)

LADY. HURF. (*Who has been deep in thought.*) Edgard, the situation is grave—

LORD EDGARD. I know. According to the *Times,* the Empire—

LADY HURF. No, no, here.

LORD EDGARD. (*Looking round him anxiously*) Here?

LADY HURF. Listen to me. We have two tender creatures in our care. Intrigues are fermenting—marriages are brewing. Personally I can't keep track of them—it gives me the vertigo. Who is to uncover them, Edgard, who is to supervise them?

LORD EDGARD. Who?

LADY HURF. Juliette is a scatterbrain. Eva is a scatterbrain. As for me, I haven't a notion what's going on and the mere idea of it bores me to extinction. Besides, I've no more commonsense than those two senseless girls. That leaves you in the midst of these three scatterbrains.

LORD EDGARD. That leaves me.

LADY HURF. Which is another way of saying nobody. I am perplexed, excessively perplexed. Anything may happen in this watering-place. Intrigues spring up under one's very feet like so much jungle vegetation. Should we do better to leave Vichy, I wonder? Ought we perhaps to bury ourselves in some rustic backwater? Edgard, for heaven's sake say something! You are the guardian of these two young things, aren't you?

LORD EDGARD. We might ask Dupont-Dufort his advice. He seems to be a man of character.

LADY HURF. A deal too much character. What a ninny you are. He's the last man from whom we want advice. The Dupont-Duforts are after our money.

LORD EDGARD. But they're rich.

LADY HURF. Exactly. That's what worries me. They're after a lot of money. An investment or a marriage settlement. Our two little ones with their millions are exceptionally tempting morsels.

LORD EDGARD. Could we not telegraph to England?

LADY HURF. What for?

LORD HURF. Scotland Yard might send us a detective.

LADY HURF. That would be a great help, I must say! They're crooked as corkscrews, the lot of them!

LORD EDGARD. The problem, then, is in effect insoluble.

LADY HURF. Edgard, you simply must bestir yourself. Our fate, the girls' and mine, is in your hands.

LORD EDGARD. *(Looks at his hands, very worried.)* I don't know that I am very well equipped.

LADY HURF. *(Sternly.)* Edgard, do you call yourself a man? And a gentleman?

LORD EDGARD. Yes.

LADY HURF. Then make a decision!

LORD EDGARD. *(Firmly.)* Very well! I shall nevertheless summon a detective from Scotland Yard, with a special proviso that I want him honest.

LADY HURF. Over my dead body! If he's honest, he'll philander with the kitchen-maids and he won't wash. It will be insufferable. And yet I don't know why I should be telling you all this. What do I want with absolute security? I'm as bored as a piece of old carpet!

LORD EDGARD. Oh, my dear—!

LADY HURF. That's all I am, a piece of old carpet.

LORD EDGARD. You, who were once so beautiful.

LADY HURF. Yes, in the nineteen-hundreds. Oh, I could scream with rage! I want to enjoy my last few years—I want to laugh a little. Sixty years I've spent deluded into thinking life a serious business. That's sixty years too long. I am in the mood, Edgard, for a gigantic piece of folly.

LORD EDGARD. Nothing dangerous, I hope?

LADY HURF. I don't know. I'll see what occurs to me. *(She leans towards him.)* I think I should like to massacre the Dupont-Duforts.

(In they come, accompanied by their particular little tune, with EVA and JULIETTE.)

D.D. SENIOR. How are you today, milady?

D.D. JUNIOR. Milady.

D.D. SENIOR. Ah, dear Lord Edgard.

LORD EDGARD. *(Drawing him aside)* Take the greatest possible care.

D.D. SENIOR. But why, milord?

LORD EDGARD. Hush! I can't tell you. But take care. Leave Vichy.

D.D. JUNIOR. We ran into these ladies on the promenade.

EVA. Vichy's an impossible place. Nothing to do, nowhere to go, and all the men are hideous.

D.D. JUNIOR. Oh, how true! Quite, quite hideous, all of them!

D.D. SENIOR. All of them! *(Aside to his son.)* Excellent thing for us.

EVA. I have an engagement tonight, Aunt. I shall be late for dinner—if I'm back at all.

D.D. SENIOR. *(Aside to his son.)* With you?

D.D. JUNIOR. No.

JULIETTE. Eva, I haven't told you. I rescued a little boy who fell into the Thermes Fountain, and I met an enchanting young man, who helped me to save him.

LADY HURF. Juliette talks of nothing else.

(The DUPONT-DUFORTS *look at each other anxiously.)*

D.D. SENIOR. Wasn't that you?

D.D. JUNIOR. No.

JULIETTE. We sat in the sun till we were dry, and chatted. You've no idea how pleasant he was! He's slight, with dark hair and—he's not the same as yours by any chance?

EVA. No. Mine's tall, with red hair.

JULIETTE. Thank goodness!

D.D. SENIOR. *(Whispers.)* Sonny, you have absolutely *got* to sparkle. *(Raising his voice)* Didier, dear boy, have you been to the swimming-pool with these ladies yet? You must give them a demonstration of your impeccable crawl. You could have rescued the toddler with the greatest of ease.

JULIETTE. Oh, the crawl would have been quite useless. The Thermes Fountain is only eighteen inches deep.

(Towards the end of this scene, PETERBONO, *as a very noble—all too noble—old Spanish gentleman,* HECTOR *as a Grandee, an equally spectacular achievement, and* GUSTAVE, *their ecclesiastical secretary, come in and slowly approach the others.)*

PETERBONO. Careful. This is big game. Stay close, and take no risks.

HECTOR. Your monocle.

PETERBONO. The big act, "Noblesse oblige." Wait for the word go. Gustave, two paces behind.

(The CLARINET strikes up a march, heroic and ultra-Spanish. Suddenly, LADY HURF, who has been watching this curious trio, runs to them and throws her arms round PETERBONO's neck.)

LADY HURF. Why, if it isn't that dear dear Duke of Miraflores!

(MUSIC stops.)

PETERBONO. *(Surprised and uneasy.)* Uh?

LADY HURF. Don't say you've forgotten! Biarritz 1902. The luncheon parties at Pampeluna! The bull-fights! Lady Hurf.

PETERBONO. Ah—! Lady Hurf. Bull-fights. Lunch. Dear friend. *(To the other two.)* I must have made up like one of her acquaintances.

LADY HURF. I am so, so happy! I was disintegrating with boredom. But where is the Duchess?

PETERBONO. Dead.

(TREMOLO from the orchestra.)

LADY HURF. Oh, heavens! And your cousin the Count?

PETERBONO. Dead.

(TREMOLO from the orchestra.)

LADY HURF. Oh, heavens! And your friend, the Admiral?

PETERBONO. Also dead.

(The ORCHESTRA begins a funeral march.)
(PETERBONO *turns to his friends.)* Saved!

LADY HURF. My poor friend. So many funerals.

PETERBONO. Alas! However, may I present my son, Don Hector? And my ecclesiastical secretary, Dom Petrus?

LADY HURF. Lord Edgard, whom you knew years ago. It was he whom you beat each morning at golf, and who was always losing his golf-balls.

PETERBONO. Ha, golf—yes. Dear friend.

LORD EDGARD. *(Panic-stricken, to* LADY HURF.*)* But, my dear—

LADY HURF. *(Sternly.)* What's the matter? Do you mean to say you don't remember the Duke?

LORD EDGARD. This is insane. Come now, think back—

LADY HURF. Your memory is abominable. Don't say another word or I shall lose my temper. My nieces, Eva and Juliette, who worry me so dreadfully because they're both very marriageable, and their dowries are exceptionally tempting to fortune-hunters.

(The DUPONT-DUFORTS *look at each other.)*

D.D. SENIOR. Dignity, lad, dignity.

D.D. JUNIOR. She can't mean us.

*(*PETERBONO *and* HECTOR *indulge in violent nudging.)*

LADY HURF. I am so delighted to have met you again. Vichy is such a dull hole. Tell me, do you remember the Ridottos on the Riviera?

PETERBONO. I should think I do!

D.D. JUNIOR. *(To his father.)* We're forgotten.

D.D. SENIOR. Let's introduce ourselves. Dupont-Dufort, senior.

D.D. JUNIOR. Junior.

(During the introductions, EVA *stares hard at* HECTOR, *who simulates an enormous interest in the conversation.* GUSTAVE *has all but disappeared into his brief case, and rummages feverishly among his papers to avoid* JULIETTE'S *gaze, which is fixed on him in puzzled interest.)*

,LADY HURF. You must be as bored as I am. It's an undreamed of stroke of fortune, our meeting, don't you think?

PETERBONO. *(Nudging* HECTOR*)* Undreamed of.

HECTOR. *(Nudging* PETERBONO) Yes. Undreamed of—absolutely undreamed of.

(In their glee, they go much too far, but no one seems to notice.)

LADY HURF. Your son is most charming. Don't you think so, Eva?

EVA. Yes.

PETERBONO. He was the most dashing officer in the entire Spanish army—before the revolution.

LADY HURF. Alas! You suffered a great deal?

PETERBONO. A great deal.

LADY HURF. Where are you staying? Not at an hotel?

PETERBONO. *(Vaguely.)* Yes.

LADY HURF. It's out of the question, Edgard! The Duke is staying at an hotel!

LORD EDGARD. But, my dearest, I assure you—

LADY HURF. Be quiet! Dear Duke, you cannot, you simply cannot stay at an hotel. Will you do us the honour of accepting our humble hospitality? Our villa is enormous, and we shall put the west wing entirely at your disposal.

PETERBONO. Certainly, certainly, certainly, certainly—

(Stupendous nudging between PETERBONO *and* HECTOR. *The* DUPONT-DUFORTS *exchange crestfallen glances.)*

LADY HURD. You may, needless to say, bring your entourage. *(She looks enquiringly at* GUSTAVE.) Is he looking for something?

PETERBONO. A document, yes. Dom Petrus!

GUSTAVE. *(Emerging from the brief-case)* Your Grace? *(He has put on some dark glasses.)*

LADY HURF. Has he got bad eyes?

PETERBONO. Oh, very bad. His condition requires a certain amount of care. I couldn't burden you with his presence. Dom Petrus, we shall accept Lady Hurf's generous offer of hospitality. Call at the hotel, will you, and have our luggage sent on. And stay there until further notice. You will collect the mail and come to us each morning for instructions.

GUSTAVE. *(Furious.)* But, your Grace—

PETERBONO. Enough!

GUSTAVE. Your Grace—

PETERBONO. Off with you!

(HECTOR gives GUSTAVE a push, and he wanders reluctantly away.)

LADY HURF. *(Moved.)* Just as he used to be! That same commanding tone—the vocal magic of the Miraflores! Your cousin had it too.

PETERBONO. Alas!

LADY HURF. How did he die?

PETERBONO. Er, how he died?

LADY HUFF. Yes—I was so fond of him.

PETERBONO. You want me to relate the circumstances of his passing?

LADY HURF. Yes.

PETERBONO. *(Turns to HECTOR in his panic.)* Well, he died—

(HECTOR mimes a motor accident, but this PETROBONO cannot grasp.)

PETERBONO. He died insane.

LADY HURF. Ah, poor fellow! He always was eccentric. But your wife, the dear Duchess?

PETERBONO. Dead.

LADY HURF. Yes, I know. But how?

(HECTOR touches his heart several times. PETERBONO is slow to take the suggestion, but as he has no imagination whatever himself, he gives way.)

PETERBONO. Of love.

LADY HURF. *(In confusion.)* Oh, I beg your pardon! And your friend the Admiral?

PETERBONO. Ah, now the Admiral—

(He looks at HECTOR, who indicates that he has run out of ideas. He again misinterprets the pantomime.)

Drowned. But please excuse me, you are re-opening wounds which time has not yet healed.

LADY HURF. Oh, forgive me, dear friend, forgive me! *(To the* OTHERS.) What breeding! What grandeur in adversity! Don't you think so, Edgard?

LORD EDGARD. My dear, I still insist that—

LADY HURF. Do stop insisting. Can't you see the Duke is suffering?

D.D. SENIOR. *(To his son.)* Let us join in the conversation.

D.D. JUNIOR. What an appalling avalanche of misfortunes!

D.D. SENIOR. Falling on such venerable heads!

(No one listens.)

LADY HURF. *(In a peal of laughter.)* How beautiful Biarritz was in those days. Do you remember the balls?

PETERBONO. Ah, the balls—

LADY HURF. And Lina Veri?

PETERBONO. Lina Veri. I can't quite recall—

LADY HURF. Come, come. Why, you were intimate! *(To the* OTHERS.) He's aged so much.

PETERBONO. Oh, Lina Veri. Of course. The darling of Italian society.

LADY HURF. No, no, no. She was a dancer.

PETERBONO. Oh yes, but her mother was the darling of Italian society.

LADY HURF. *(To the* OTHERS.) He's wandering a little. He's very tired. My dear Duke, I would like to show you your apartments right away. The villa is close by, at the end of the avenue.

PETERBONO. With pleasure.

*(*GUSTAVE *comes running in, this time as his own charming self, but magnificently dressed.)*

GUSTAVE. Good morning, Father!

PETERBONO. *(Off his balance.)* Little basket! Allow me to present my second son, Don Pedro, whom I'd forgotten to mention.

LADY HURF. Gracious, you have another son? By whom?

PETERBONO. *(Panicking again)* Ah, that's a long story— *(He looks at HECTOR, who signs to him to go carefully.)*
But that one also opens wounds as yet unhealed by time.

LADY HURF. Come along, Edgard.

LORD EDGARD. But, my dear—

LADY HURF. And keep quiet!

(They go, HECTOR paying elaborate attentions to EVA, who has continued to stare at him.)

JULIETTE. *(To GUSTAVE.)* Now will you kindly tell me what is going on?

GUSTAVE. Ssh! I'll explain later.

(They go too. The DUPONT-DUFORTS are left alone.)

D.D. JUNIOR. Father, they've forgotten us—!

D.D. SENIOR. All the same, we'll follow. And, Didier, twice the affability. Let's hope these young men are already attached or better still that they aren't interested in women!

(They go.)

ACT TWO

A drawing-room in LADY HURF'S *house. It is evening, after dinner, and* JULIETTE *and* GUSTAVE *are sitting side by side; a little romantic air is heard in the distance.*

JULIETTE. It's nice here. No one is disturbing us tonight.
GUSTAVE. Yes, it is nice.
JULIETTE. For three days now you've been sad. Are you homesick for Spain?
GUSTAVE. Oh no.
JULIETTE. I'm sorry now I wouldn't work at my Spanish at school. We might have spoken it together. It would have been fun.
GUSTAVE. I only speak a few words myself.
JULIETTE. Do you? That's funny.
GUSTAVE. Yes, it is rather.

(A silence.)

JULIETTE. It must be amusing to be a prince.
GUSTAVE. Oh, one gets used to it, you know.

(A silence.)

JULIETTE. Don Pedro, what's the matter? We were much friendlier three days ago.
GUSTAVE. Nothing's the matter.

(A pause. LORD EDGARD *crosses the room laden with papers.)*

LORD EDGARD. *(Muttering)* Though I should die in the endeavour, I'll set my mind at rest. *(He drops his papers.)*
    (They jump up to help him but he bars their path.) Don't touch them! Don't touch them! *(He picks up the papers himself and goes out muttering.)* This momentous discovery, if discovery there must be, must be surrounded with the greatest possible precautions.

GUSTAVE. What is he looking for? He's done nothing but ferret about among those old papers since we came here.

JULIET. I don't know. He's a little mad. Only he's painstaking as well, you see, so sometimes the results are quite prodigious.

(A LITTLE GIRL *comes in.)*
Oh, here's my little friend.

CHILD. Mademoiselle Juliette, I've picked some daisies for you.

JULIETTE. Thank you, darling.

CHILD. They haven't many petals. Daddy says they aren't the ones that lovers use.

JULIETTE. Never mind.

CHILD. Shall I get some others?

JULIETTE. No. Yes. You're very sweet. *(She kisses her.)* Run away now.

(The CHILD *goes.)*
*(*JULIETTE *turns to* GUSTAVE, *shamefaced.)* Do you think it's silly of me?

GUSTAVE. No.

JULIETTE. You said you loved me, Don Pedro, yet for three days now you haven't even looked at me.

GUSTAVE. I do love you, Juliette.

JULIETTE. Then why—?

GUSTAVE. I can't tell you.

JULIETTE. My father wasn't titled, I know, but my aunt is a Lady, and my grandfather was an Honourable.

GUSTAVE. How funny you are. It isn't that.

JULIETTE. Do you think the Duke of Miraflores would consent to my marrying you?

GUSTAVE. *(Smiling)* I'm sure he would.

JULIETTE. Why do you look so sad then, if you love me and everyone approves?

GUSTAVE. I can't tell you.

JULIETTE. But you do feel, don't you, that our lives might meet and join one day?

GUSTAVE. I would be lying if I told you I felt that.

JULIETTE. *(Turning away)* That's unkind of you.

GUSTAVE. Careful. Here's your cousin.

JULIET. Come into the garden. It's getting dark. I want you to tell me everything.

(The MUSIC fades as they go. EVA comes in, followed by HECTOR, in a totally different make-up from the one he wore in Act I.)

HECTOR. There, you see, they've left us the place to ourselves.

EVA. But I don't in the least need a place to myself—that's the pity of it—I could adapt myself quite easily to a great crowd around us.

HECTOR. How cruel you are!

EVA. I don't like you. I'm cruel to those I dislike. It's in my nature. But on the other hand, when someone appeals to me, there's hardly anything I wouldn't do for him.

HECTOR. *(In despair.)* Why, why can I not manage to appeal to you a second time?

EVA. You know perfectly well why. You're not the same now.

HECTOR. What abominable absent-mindedness! This disguise, I tell you, is the fancy of an aristocrat wearied to death of his own personality, a pastime which affords him an escape from his oppressive self. And for this accursed fancy, must I lose my love?

EVA. I remember with delight a young man who spoke to me in the park. Find him for me. I might still think him lovable.

HECTOR. This is ridiculous! Won't you even tell me if I'm getting warm? At least tell me, did I have a beard when I first appealed to you?

EVA. But it wouldn't amuse me if I were to tell you.

HECTOR. *(Who has turned away to change his make-up, turns back again wearing a completely new face.)* It wasn't like this, I suppose?

EVA. *(In a burst of laughter.)* No, oh no!

HECTOR. Yet you remember my voice, my eyes?

EVA. Yes, but it isn't enough.

HECTOR. I'm the same height as I was. I'm tall, well built—I assure you I am, very well built.

EVA. I only judge by faces.

HECTOR. This is horrible! Horrible! I'll never find the face that pleased you, ever! It wasn't as a woman, by any chance?

EVA. What do you take me for?

HECTOR. Or as a Chinaman?

EVA. You're evidently out of your mind. I'll wait till you're in it again.

(She goes to sit further off; he starts to follow her and she turns on him.)

No, no, no! For heaven's sake will you stop following me about and changing your beard every five minutes! You're making my head spin.

HECTOR. *(Stricken.)* And to think that idiot Peterbono keeps on swearing it was as a test-pilot!

(LORD EDGARD crosses the room laden with papers.)

LORD EDGARD. This is unthinkable! I must find this letter, from which the truth will spring in such a curious fashion.

(He sees HECTOR in his latest make-up, drops his papers and leaps on him.)

At last! The detective from Scotland Yard.

HECTOR. No sir. *(He makes to go.)*

LORD EDGARD. Excellent! The perfect answer. I specially stipulated secrecy. But don't be afraid, I am Lord Edgard in person. You may disclose your identity.

HECTOR. I tell you I'm not the man you're expecting. *(He goes.)*

LORD EDGARD. *(Following him)* I see! I see! Perfect! You're keeping word for word to my instructions! I stressed the need for caution!

(LADY HURF enters, holding a magazine.)

LADY HURF. My little Eva is bored, isn't she?

(EVA smiles and says nothing. Unseen by LADY HURF, HECTOR comes back in another make-up, which he

silently shows EVA. *She shakes her head and he retires, heavy-hearted.* LADY HURF *puts down her magazine with a sigh.)*

LADY HURF. My little Eva is as bored as she can be.

EVA. *(With a smile.)* Yes, Aunt.

LADY HURF. So am I, darling, very bored.

EVA. Only I'm twenty-five, so you see, it's rather sad.

LADY HURF. You'll see how much sadder it can be when you are sixty. For you there's always love. As you may guess, it's several years now since I officially renounced it.

EVA. Oh, love!

LADY HURF. *What* a deep sigh! Since you've been a widow, surely you've had lovers?

EVA. I never had a single one who loved me.

LADY HURF. You want the moon. If your lovers bore you, marry one of them. That will give the others an added fascination.

EVA. Marry? Whom?

LADY HURF. Needless to say these Dupont-Duforts exasperate us both. What about the Spaniards?

EVA. Prince Hector chases after me changing his moustache in the hope of rediscovering the one that first appealed to me.

LADY HURF. Truly appealed to you?

EVA. *(Smiling)* I don't remember.

LADY HURF. They're curious individuals.

EVA. Why?

LADY HURF. Oh, I don't know. I tell you, I'm an old carcass who doesn't know what to do with herself. I've had everything a woman could reasonably, or even unreasonably, wish for. Money, power, lovers. Now that I'm old, I feel as alone inside my skin as I did as a little girl and they made me face the wall when I'd been naughty. And here's the rub; I know that between that little girl and this old woman, there has been, under the charivari and the noise, nothing but an even greater loneliness.

EVA. I've always thought of you as happy.

LADY HURF. You don't see much, do you? I am playing a part. Only, like everything else I do, I play it well, that's all. Yours now, you play badly, little girl. *(She strokes her hair.)* Child, child, you will always find yourself pursued by desires with changing beards and never have the courage to tell one of them: stay as you are—I love you. Don't think yourself a martyr now. All women are the same. My little Juliette, though, will come through because she is romantic. Her simplicity will save her. It's a favour only granted to few.

EVA. There are some who can love.

LADY HURF. Yes. There are some who love a man. Who kill him with loving, who kill themselves for him, but they are seldom heiresses to millions. *(She strokes her hair again, with a rueful smile.)* Ah, you'll finish up like me, an old woman covered in diamonds who plays at intrigues in an effort to forget that she has never lived. And yet, I'd like to laugh a little. Here am I, playing with fire, and the fire won't even burn my fingers.

EVA. What do you meant, Aunt?

LADY HURF. Shush—here come our marionettes.

(PETERBONO *and* HECTOR *appear in the doorway, preceded by the* MUSICIAN, *and followed almost at once by the* DUPONT-DUFORTS. *They* ALL *rush towards the* LADIES, *but it is the* THIEVES *who get there first to kiss their hands.*)

(Jumps to her feet and utters a sudden cry.) Ah! I have an idea!

PETERBONO. *(Frightened, to* HECTOR.) She scares the life out of me. Every time she screams like that, I think my beard's loose.

LADY HURF. Where is Juliette?

EVA. In the garden, with Prince Pedro. They're inseparable.

PETERBONO. Ah, the dear children!

LADY HURF. *(Calling)* Juliette!

JULIETTE. *(Coming in with* GUSTAVE) Did you want me, Aunt Emily?

LADY HURF. *(Drawing her aside)* Your eyes are red,

child. Now mind, you mustn't be unhappy, or I cut the strings and the puppets will fall down.

JULIETTE. What do you mean, Aunt?

LADY HURF. If I appear to be talking through my hat, it's precisely so you won't understand me. Come along, both of you. *(She takes them by the waist and leads them into the garden.)* I have an idea to brighten up this evening; I want you to tell me what you think of it.

(They go. The DUPONT-DUFORTS *look at each other.)*

D.D. SENIOR. After them, sonny. And a hundred times more charm. Remember, it's our future that's at stake.

D.D. JUNIOR. Yes, Pa.

(Left alone, the three THIEVES *can unbend.)*

HECTOR. *(Offering* PETERBONO *a box of cigars)* Would you care for a cigar?

PETERBONO. *(Helping himself)* I'm savouring them. They're remarkably good .

HECTOR. *(Pouring out)* A little brandy?

PETERBONO. Thank you.

(They drink.)

HECTOR. Another cigar, perhaps?

PETERBONO. *(Grabbing a fistful without more ado.)* You're too kind. No, no really, you embarrass me. *(He feels a slight remorse, and takes the box.)* But may I in return press you to a cigar?

HECTOR. *(Pulling them out of his pockets in handfuls)* Thank you so much. I'm all right just now.

(There is a moment of beatitude and exquisite refinement. They spread themselves blissfully on the sofa. Suddenly HECTOR *indicates* GUSTAVE, *sitting sad and sombre in his corner.)*

PETERBONO. *(Rises and goes to him.)* What's wrong, laddie? Why so sad? Here you are with a wonderful room, lovely food, and a pretty little thing to flirt with, you're playing at princes, and for all that you can manage to be gloomy?

GUSTAVE. I don't want to stay here.

(*The* OTHER TWO *give a start.*)

PETERBONO. Uh? You want to leave?

GUSTAVE. Yes.

PETERBONO. Leave here?

GUSTAVE. Yes—leave here.

PETERBONO. Hector, the boy's lost his reason.

HECTOR. What do you want to leave for?

GUSTAVE. I'm in love with Juliette.

HECTOR. Well then?

GUSTAVE. Really in love.

HECTOR. Well then?

PETERBONO. Why not? You've never been better off. She takes you for a prince, and rich at that. Go in and win, lad, she's as good as yours.

GUSTAVE. I don't want to take her, for a day, and then be forced to leave her.

PETERBONO. You'll have to leave her one day.

GUSTAVE. And—I'm ashamed of this game I have to play with her. I'd rather go away, now, and never see her again.

HECTOR. He's out of his mind.

PETERBONO. Completely.

GUSTAVE. Look, what are we here for?

PETERBONO. What are we here for? We're working, lad. It's the height of our season.

GUSTAVE. We're here to do a job. Let's do it then and go.

PETERBONO. And the preliminaries? Have you spared a single thought for the preliminaries?

GUSTAVE. They've gone on long enough, your damn preliminaries.

PETERBONO. I ask you, Hector, isn't it painful? Having to listen to an apprentice teaching us our trade!

HECTOR. Of course we'll do a job; that's what we came

for, but have you even the first idea what that job's going
to be?

GUSTAVE. Strip the drawing-room?

PETERBONO. With carpet-bags, eh? Like raggle-taggle
gypsies! The lowness, Hector, the abysmal lowness of this
youngster's mind! Understand, boy, that we haven't yet
decided on the job we're going to do. And if our behaviour
strikes you, a novice, as peculiar, tell yourself it's because
we're in the process of investigating the possibilities of
this—establishment.

GUSTAVE. You're lingering on here for the brandy and
cigars, and because Hector still hopes he'll get Eva to
remember him. But in actual fact you haven't the smallest
inkling what you want to do. I may be an apprentice, but
I'll tell you something—that's no way to work.

PETERBONO. (*Running to* HECTOR) Hector hold me
back!

HECTOR. (*Still blissfully smoking.*) Gustave, don't be
difficult. Try to understand.

PETERBONO. Hector, hold me back!

HECTOR. You see, we're wavering—

PETERBONO. Hold me back, Hector! Hold me back!

HECTOR. (*Takes his arm to please him.*) All right, I've
got you.

PETERBONO. (*Deflated.*) Just as well.

HECTOR. (*To* GUSTAVE.) We're wavering between several possible courses of action—

GUSTAVE. Which?

HECTOR. Shall we confide in him, Pete? Is it safe to risk
the indiscretion of a youth?

PETERBONO. (*Shrugs.*) Oh, confide in him, do. Since
we're answerable to him now.

HECTOR. Right. Tell him your idea first, Pete.

PETERBONO. After you, Hector, after you.

HECTOR. (*Embarrassed.*) Aaaaaaah—well—

GUSTAVE. You haven't thought of a thing!

HECTOR. (*In righteous rage.*) We haven't thought of a
thing?!!! We're wavering between the trick of the dud
cheque given in exchange for real jewels on a Saturday,

which gives the weekend to make our getaway, or the trick of the good cheque received in exchange for dud jewels under the same conditions. We've also considered giving Lady Hurf some orchids sprayed with ether (taking good care not to smell them ourselves) so as to relieve her of the pearls as soon as she nods off.

PETERBONO. *(Equally incensed.)* Or we might provoke the Dupont-Duforts to a duel! We wound them and then in the commotion we make off with the silver!

GUSTAVE. What if you're the ones to get wounded?

PETERBONO. Impossible!

GUSTAVE. Why?

PETERBONO. *(Yelling)* I don't know. But it's impossible!

HECTOR. Or again we could make out we'd been robbed and demand a colossal sum for hush-money!

PETERBONO. Pretend we found a pearl in the oysters at dinner, for instance, and swap it for a pearl of Lady Hurf's, or something.

GUSTAVE. There's no "r" in the month.

PETERBONO. I said for instance!

GUSTAVE. In other words you just don't know. Well, I'm going to do the job tonight, and then I'm off.

PETERBONO. Tonight? And why not right away?

GUSTAVE. Yes, why not right away? I want to go away. I want to leave here as soon as possible.

PETERBONO. He'll be the ruin of us! Gustave, think of your poor old mother, who put you in my care!

GUSTAVE. No!

PETERBONO. I'll put my curse on you! Naturally you don't care a rap if I put my curse on you?

GUSTAVE. No.

PETERBONO. *(Bellowing)* Hector! Hold me back! *(He seizes GUSTAVE.)* Just another fortnight. We'll do the job all right, but it's nice here, and it isn't so often we're in a nice place—

GUSTAVE. No. I'm too unhappy. *(He goes.)*

HECTOR. *(Leaps after him.)* After him! We've got to stop him before he starts a scandal.

PETERBONO. *(Calling after him)* I've got an idea! Suppose we pretended not to know him?

(HECTOR *shrugs his shoulders and goes out, refusing even to consider such a solution. Enter* LORD EDGARD, *preceded by the* MUSICIAN *playing a succession of tremolos as if he had intimations of a sudden blow of destiny. He is rummaging in his ever-present pile of papers. All of a sudden he utters a loud cry and falls in a dead faint among his scattered letters. The* MUSICIAN *runs for help, emitting isolated notes from his instrument.)*

JULIETTE. *(Comes in.)* Uncle, Uncle, what's the matter? *(She props him up on a sofa and feels his hands.)* Ice-cold! What's this? *(She picks up a letter; reads it, and hurriedly thrusts it into her pocket. Running out)* Aunt Emily! Aunt Emily! Come quickly!

(The MUSICIAN *in great confusion multiplies his tragic tremolos.* EVERYONE *comes rushing in, shouting at once:)*

Stroke!
At his age!
No, he's only fainted.
Stand back—give him air.
Get a doctor!
He's coming round.
He's all right now.
A sudden shock.
Perhaps he found what he was looking for.

(The MUSIC stops. An enormous silence.)

PETERBONO. *(Breathes to* HECTOR *in the silence.)* The chance of a lifetime.

HECTOR. Yes. But what do we do about it?

PETERBONO. Well, nothing, obviously, but it's still the chance of a lifetime.

LORD EDGARD. *(Sitting up slowly, says in a toneless*

voice) My friends, I have a ghastly piece of news for you. The Duke of Miraflores died in Biarritz in 1904.

(EVERYONE *looks at* PETERBORO, *who is very ill at ease. An impish little JIG on the clarinet.*)

PETERBONO. Nonsense!

HECTOR. *(Aside.)* Talk about the chance of a lifetime!

PETERBONO. This is a fine time to be funny! Ease over to the window.

LADY HURF. Edgard, are you out of your mind?

LORD EDGARD. No, I tell you. I've found the notification. I knew I'd find it eventually. Ever since the day— *(He searches himself.)* Where is it? This is too much! Where is it? I had it a moment ago! Oh, my goodness! It's gone again.

D.D. SENIOR. Everything is coming to light!

D.D. JUNIOR. We are saved. *(To* PETERBORO, *who is imperceptibly edging towards the window.)* Aren't you staying to make sure your host is all right?

PETERBONO. Yes, oh yes!

LADY HURF. Edgard, that's a ridiculous joke to play on the dear Duke.

LORD EDGARD. But, my dear, I guarantee—

LADY HURF. Come along, dear Duke, and show him you aren't dead.

PETERBONO. *(Uneasy.)* No, no. I'm not dead.

LORD EDGARD. Yet I found the notification—

LADY HURF. *(Pinching him)* Edgard, you're making a mistake, I'm sure. You must apologize.

LORD EDGARD. *(Rubbing his arm)* Ouch! Why yes, now that you mention it, I think I must have been confusing him with the Duke of Orleans.

LADY HURF. Of course. Shall we call the incident closed?

PETERBONO. *(In great relief.)* Completely closed.

LADY HURF. Let's go outside, shall we? I've ordered coffee on the terrace. I want to tell you about my idea.

D.D. SENIOR. *(In step with her.)* I think it's a wonderful idea.

LADY HURF. *(Exasperated.)* Wait a minute, my dear

man, I haven't told you yet. Listen. They're holding a Thieves' Carnival tonight at the Casino. We're all going to dress up as thieves and go to it.

D.D. SENIOR *and* JUNIOR. *(Immediately burst out laughing.)* He! He! He! How terribly, terribly amusing!

D.D. SENIOR. *(To his son as they go out.)* Play up to her, Son. *(Exits.)*

PETERBONO. *(Furious, as he goes out with* HECTOR.) I call that in very poor taste, don't you?

(JULIETTE *is alone. She stands motionless a moment. The MUSIC is heard some way away, playing a romantic theme.* JULIETTE *takes out the fatal letter and reads it.)*

JULIETTE. "We regret to announce the sad death of His Serene Highness the Duke of Miraflores y Grandes, Marquis of Priola, Count of Zeste and Galba. The funeral will take place—" *(She stands in thought a moment.)* If his father isn't the Duke of Miraflores—then who can he be? Why has he taken the car out of the garage? Why is he hiding from me?

CHILD. *(Entering)* Mademoiselle Juliette, I found some. Look, daisies with lots of petals.

JULIETTE. Haven't you gone to bed yet?

CHILD. I was picking daisies for you.

JULIETTE. Thank you, you're an angel. *(She kisses her.)* His father may be an adventurer, but you see, he loves me. He does love me, doesn't he?

CHILD. Yes, of course he does.

JULIETTE. We don't care, do we, if he's an adventurer, or worse? If you were me, you'd love him, wouldn't you, just the same? Only why does that hard look come into his eyes whenever I ask him about himself? If he has designs on me, and he'd be wise to have, because I'm very rich, he should be very pleasant to me all the time—whereas—do you think he prefers Eva? That would be terrible—

CHILD. I don't know.

JULIETTE. No, of course you don't. Come along, I'll take you home. Are you afraid of the dark?

CHILD. No.

JULIETTE. That's a good girl. Nor am I. There's nothing to be afraid of, you know. Thieves won't hurt you.

(They go.)

ACT THREE

The same set. The room is dark; a FIGURE *is seen moving about with a torch. It is* GUSTAVE, *dressed in dark clothes and wearing a cap. He is silently examining the objects in the drawing-room. Suddenly he hears a noise and switches off the torch; a low whistle; two dark* FIGURES *spring up, two torches flash, and focus on* GUSTAVE.

GUSTAVE. Who's that?

FIGURE. Tonight's the night.

GUSTAVE. Peterbono?

FIGURE. No. We're the new ones.

2ND FIGURE. The new bandits.

GUSTAVE. For God's sake, what's going on? *(He draws a revolver.)* Hands up!

D.D. SENIOR. *(It is no other.)* Ha ha ha! That's good! Where did you get the gun? It's magnificent!

GUSTAVE. Stay where you are or I fire!

D.D. SENIOR. Come quietly! The game's up.

GUSTAVE. Stay where you are, damn you! *(He fires.)*

D.D. SENIOR. *(Blissfully unaware of his danger.)* Oh, well done! Bravo!

GUSTAVE. What do you mean, bravo? *(He fires again.)*

D.D. JUNIOR. It's a wonderful imitation! Where on earth did you buy those caps?

GUSTAVE. For the last time, stay where you are! *(He fires again and shatters a vase, which falls with a terrible clatter.)*

D.D. SENIOR. Didier, why do you have to be so clumsy!

D.D. JUNIOR. *(Protesting in the dark)* But, Dad, I didn't do it!

D.D. SENIOR. Well, it can't have been I, can it? I'm in the middle of the room.

D.D. JUNIOR. But, Dad, so am I!

D.D. SENIOR. *(Suddenly anxious.)* Well, then, who broke the vase?

37

LORD EDGARD. *(Enters and switches on the LIGHT. He is dressed up as a policeman.)* Now, now, what is all this noise? How do you like my helmet?

D.D. SENIOR. *(Who has got himself up, along with his son, in a terrifying apache disguise.)* Superb; my lord, superb!

(Exit LORD EDGARD.*)*

(D.D. SENIOR *goes to* GUSTAVE.) My word, I don't think much of your costume. It doesn't come off—it's much too simple. It's the little touches that mean so much. For instance, look, this little scar here.

D.D. JUNIOR. And the black eye patch.

GUSTAVE. What are you doing dressed up like that?

D.D. SENIOR. We're going to the Casino.

D.D. JUNIOR. To the Thieves' Carnival. And so are you.

GUSTAVE. Oh? Oh yes, of course. So am I.

D.D. SENIOR. Only if I were you, I'd touch up your makeup, my boy. It's a shade too simple. You don't look a bit like a thief.

GUSTAVE. You're quite right. I'll see to it at once. *(He turns at the door.)* Tell me, is everybody going to the Thieves' Carnival?

D.D. SENIOR. Of course; everybody.

GUSTAVE. That's fine. See you later. *(He goes.)*

D.D. SENIOR. Not an ounce of imagination in him, that boy.

D.D. JUNIOR. If the other two have rigged themselves up as absurdly as that, which they probably have, we're well on the way. The girls will have eyes for nobody but us!

D.D. SENIOR. Have you seen the latest batch of telegrams?

D.D. JUNIOR. Yes.

D.D. SENIOR. If we don't leave this house with a fat settlement, it's the colonies for us, I can tell you. Make yourself irresistible, there's a good boy.

D.D. JUNIOR. I'm doing my best, Dad.

D.D. SENIOR. I know you are. You're an honest, con-

scientious lad, but you mustn't slacken for one moment.
The success of this evening's entertainment means a great
deal to us. What's more, there's something shady about
our rivals which is bound to give rise to a scandal one of
these days. It was quite obviously Lady Hurf who made
the old duffer keep quiet this afternoon, when he insisted
the Duke of Miraflores died in 1904. Keep your eyes
open, and be ready for any emergency.

D.D. JUNIOR. We have got to get rid of these gallivant-
ers. It's a matter of life and death.

D.D. SENIOR. We'll let them dig their own graves, while
we'll be more and more agreeable. Ssh! Here comes Lady
Hurf.

(Enter LADY HURF *and* EVA *as thieves in petticoats. The*
DUPONT-DUFORTS *cough desperately to attract attention.)*

LADY HURF. *(Seeing them)* Oh, breathtaking! Aren't
they, Eva? Breathtaking! Who would have thought they
had it in them! What do you think of our guests, Eva:

EVA. What a spectacular effect! How in the world did
you manage it?

D.D. SENIOR. *(Simpering)* We're delighted.

D.D. JUNIOR. That we delight you.

LADY HURF. They always look as though they're waiting for a tip.

EVA. Which, in a way, they are.

LADY HURF. The Duke and his sons are being very
slow.

EVA. I called out to them as I went by. They can't manage to dress up as thieves, they said.

LADY HURF. *(As she goes.)* Go up and fetch them,
gentlemen, if you would be so good, and give them a few
wrinkles.

D.D. SENIOR. Certainly! Certainly! *(Aside to his son.)*
Let us be pleasant.

D.D. JUNIOR. Very, very pleasant.

(They bow themselves out. JULIETTE *crosses furtively.)*

EVA. Why, you're not dressed!

JULIETTE. I'm going up now.

EVA. You'll make us late.

JULIETTE. Go on ahead. I'll take the two-seater.

EVA. *(Unexpectedly.)* Are you in love with this boy?

JULIETTE. Why do you ask me?

EVA. Yes indeed, why does one ask people if they're in love, when one can tell at a glance, always.

JULIETTE. Can you tell?

EVA. Yes.

JULIETTE. Well, you're wrong. I'm not in love with anyone.

(She turns to go, then EVA *calls her back.)*

EVA. Juliette! Why do you look upon me as your enemy?

JULIETTE. You are my enemy.

EVA. No, I love you very much. Sit down.

JULIETTE. *(Turning on her)* You're in love with him too, that's it, isn't it? You're going to take him away from me, and you want to warn me first so that I won't be hurt too much? Why, you've even agreed on that between you, probably. You have, haven't you? Haven't you? For heaven's sake say something! Why do you smile like that?

EVA. How lucky you are to be in love as much as that.

JULIETTE. You're prettier than I am; you can get any man you want.

EVA. Oh, if I could only bring myself to want one.

JULIETTE. Don't you want him then?

EVA. No, little silly.

JULIETTE. Have you never spoken to him when I wasn't looking?

EVA. Had I ever wanted to I should have found it very difficult. He only has to come near me by accident and you can't take your eyes off us.

JULIETTE. I'm wary. I love him, you see.

EVA. Little gambler!

JULIETTE. You swear you've never set out to attract him?

Eva. I swear.

Juliette. Even the day you danced with him twice running?

Eva. The orchestra had struck up a second tango.

Juliette. Even the day you went out on the river while the Dupont-Duforts tried to teach me roulette?

Eva. Even then. He looked so sad that I suggested he should row straight back, but we couldn't find you anywhere.

Juliette. That day I'm not so sure. He had a strange look in his eyes that evening.

Eva. Because he'd asked me if I thought you cared for him, and I said you were an unpredictable little girl and there was no knowing what went on inside your heart.

Juliette. Was that truly why?

(A little pause.)

All the same, I do think you might have told him something else.

Eva. Are you satisfied now?

Juliette. Did you never try to attract him, not even at the beginning, not even the very first day?

Eva. Not even the first day.

Juliette. Yes, then, I'm satisfied.

Eva. Why will you never trust me? I feel like an old woman beside you sometimes.

Juliette. You're so much better-looking than I am, so much more poised, more feminine.

Eva. Do you think so?

Juliette. It surprises me, you know, in spite of what you say. You must admit that he's a good deal more attractive than Hector, and you don't mind *his* attentions.

Eva. Do you think I couldn't have denied myself a mere flirtation, when I could see you were so much in love?

Juliette. That's grand of you.

Eva. Oh no. I wish I could have wanted him so much that I'd have sacrificed you without giving you a moment's thought.

Juliette. When you chew your pearls, I know there's something wrong.

EVA. Yes, there's something wrong.

JULIETTE. Yet you look so lovely tonight. You'll have all the men around you at the Ball.

EVA. All of them.

JULIETTE. I'm not joking.

EVA. Nor am I. I'll have them all. And yet it's very sad.

JULIETTE. Aren't you happy?

EVA. No.

JULIETTE. Yet it's so easy. You only need to let yourself go. Why, hardly a moment goes by that one isn't unhappy, yet I think that must be what it means, to be happy.

EVA. You've always thought me cleverer, stronger, more beautiful than you because the men flocked round me. And yet, you see, there's only you who is alive, in this house—you're the only one perhaps in Vichy, perhaps in the whole world.

JULIETTE. *(Smiling, lost in her dream.)* Yes, I am alive.

EVA. And untouched, and eager to believe—

JULIETTE. To believe everything.

EVA. You've never had, as I have, a man without love in your bed. You haven't even a jewel at your throat, not a ring on your finger. You're wearing nothing but this simple linen dress, and you're twenty years old, and you are in love.

(JULIETTE *sits motionless, yielding to the unseen with a faint smile.*)

(Looking sharply at her) Juliette, why are you not in thieves' dress like the rest of us?

JULIETTE. *(Bursting with sudden joy)* Oh, I'm too happy! I haven't the courage to stay beside you who are sad. When I'm a little less happy, I'll think of you, I swear I will! *(She kisses her and runs off.)* Ssh!

EVA. All this mystery! What are you trying to say?

(*Enter* LADY HURF *with the* DUPONT-DUFORTS.)

LADY HURF. We will make a truly magnificent entrance.

D.D. SENIOR. The Spanish gentlemen are ready.

LADY HURF. Do they look all right?

D.D. SENIOR. That's a matter of taste.

D.D. JUNIOR. Anyway, here they come.

(Enter PETERBONO *and* HECTOR. *They have contrived to disguise themselves as absolutely ludicrous comic opera bandits. They are greeted with shrieks of laughter.)*

HECTOR. What are they laughing at?

PETERBONO. What do they *think* thieves look like? Don't they ever go to the theatre?

LADY HURF. But, my dear Duke, what are you supposed to be?

PETERBONO. A thief.

HECTOR. *(To* EVA.) It wasn't like this, I suppose?

EVA. Heavens, no!

PETERBONO. *(To* LADY HURF.) Don't you like us?

LADY HURF. Enormously!

PETERBONO. Admit there's something wrong.

LADY HURF. My dear friend, one really can't expect a Spanish grandee to make much of a showing as a common thief.

PETERBONO. Well said, eh, Hector? *(Enormous nudgings.)*

LADY HURF. Come along, all of you. The car's waiting. Where is Lord Edgard? Still glued to the mirror I suppose. Edgard!

(He appears, still in his own suit, and wearing his police helmet, but he has shaved off his moustache.)

LORD EDGARD. Do you think I did well to shave off my moustache?

LADY HURF. *(Without looking at him)* I don't know! Come along! To the Carnival!

(The MUSIC immediately strikes up a lively quadrille, which the THIEVES *dance to with the* LADIES, *without the* DUPONT-DUFORTS *getting a look-in. Then follows a piece of extremely vulgar jive, and the* DUPONT-DUFORTS, *making the best of a bad job,*

*finish up by dancing together with tremendous spirit.
ALL dance their way out.)*

D.D. SENIOR. *(Bringing up the rear with his son)*
Things are getting better and better and better.

D.D. JUNIOR. Let's be as witty as the very devil!

D.D. SENIOR. And remember, Didier, twice as nice.

*(The room remains empty for an instant. A SERVANT
comes in to close the windows and turn out the lights.
Another moment of silence, and GUSTAVE appears,
an listens. The CAR is heard driving off. He goes
right round the room, examining its contents one
by one. All of a sudden he flattens himself against
the wall.)*

JULIETTE. *(Enters, dressed for a journey.)* Here I am.

GUSTAVE. What are you doing here? Why didn't you
go with the others?

JULIETTE. I've come to find you.

GUSTAVE. Get out of here, will you?

JULIETTE. Why are you so harsh with me?

GUSTAVE. Go on, get out!

JULIETTE. I'll go, of course, if you don't want me, only
I thought you would want me. What's the matter?

GUSTAVE. I've got a headache. I want to stay here.

JULIETTE. Why this yarn, to me?

GUSTAVE. It isn't a yarn. Get out, will you. Go on,
quick march!

JULIETTE. But—you've never spoken to me like this!

GUSTAVE. There's a first time for everything.

JULIETTE. What have I done?

GUSTAVE. Nothing in particular. It's too difficult to
explain, and anyway you wouldn't understand.

JULIETTE. But, Señor Pedro—

GUSTAVE. There isn't any Señor Pedro, for a start. My
name is Gustave. And secondly, will you please go away?

JULIETTE. And there was I thinking that you loved
me—

GUSTAVE. We all make mistakes, don't we?

JULIETTE. But you used to tell me so.

GUSTAVE. I was lying.

JULIETTE. Oh, no! I don't believe it!

GUSTAVE. *(Going to her purposefully)* Listen, my little pet, I'm telling you to get out of here, double quick.

JULIETTE. Why?

GUSTAVE. You'll see why later on. In the meantime go up to your room and weep over your lost illusions. *(He takes her arm to lead her to the door.)* What are you dressed up in this coat for? What kind of a costume is that meant to be?

JULIETTE. Travelling costume.

GUSTAVE. Travelling costume? You're mad.

JULIETTE. Please don't be angry. I came to find you so we could go away. You told me once we'd go away together.

GUSTAVE. I was joking. Anyway, how do you know I mean to go away?

JULIETTE. I know.

GUSTAVE. You look as though you know a lot of things. Come along with me.

JULIETTE. We might meet one of the servants in the passage.

(He looks at her.)

We'd better not move from here. We'll be quite safe in this room.

GUSTAVE. The Dupont-Duforts must be waiting for you. Go and dress up as a pickpocket like the rest of them.

JULIETTE. Don't pickpockets ever wear travelling clothes?

GUSTAVE. You're not going to travel. You're going to a carnival.

JULIETTE. Once they've stolen, thieves go away as a rule. Why won't you let me come with you, since you're going away?

GUSTAVE. *(Seizes her.)* You know too much, my girl!

JULIETTE. Oh, please, don't hurt me!

GUSTAVE. Don't be afraid. Just a precaution. *(He ties her to a chair, and searches in her handbag.)*

JULIETTE. Oh, don't rob my bag. There's nothing in it. Anyway, I give it to you.

GUSTAVE. Thank you. All I want is a handkerchief.

JULIETTE. What for?

GUSTAVE. To gag you with. *(He finds her handkerchief, which is microscopic.)* I ask you, what's the point of a handkerchief that size? Never mind, mine's clean.

JULIETTE. I'm not going to scream—I swear I won't scream—Señor Pedro! Gustave—Gusta—

GUSTAVE. *(He gags her.)* There. If you think this a Thieves' Carnival, my lass, you'll have to think again. I'm a real thief, I am. So is Hector, and so is the Duke of Miraflores. Except that those two, they're imbeciles as well. You've built yourself a castle in the air, that's all, and your aunt, who's got bats in her belfry, has built herself a dozen. But let me tell you *I* came to do a job, and I intend to do it.

(She struggles.)

All right. All right. It's no good trying to soften me. I'm used to girls. *(He begins to fill his sacks with the most unlikely objects in the room. After a while he looks at her with misgiving.)* It's not too tight, is it?

(She shakes her head.)

That's a good girl. You see, old girl, I did a bit of billing and cooing, I know, but to be frank I didn't mean a word of it. I had to do it for the job.

(She struggles again.)

Does that upset you? Yes, I know, it isn't very pretty. But then in every trade there's always a little bit like that which isn't very pretty. Apart from that, I'm an honest sort of chap in my own way. I follow my trade, simply, without frills and fancies. Not like Hector and Peterbono. Peterbono has to be the Duke of Miraflores. One must be honest in one's own particular line. Life's not worth living otherwise. *(He takes a furtive look at her.)* You sure it's not too tight? *(He gives her a smile.)* It worries me a bit, playing a trick like that on you, because you know, I lied just now. I am fond of you really. *(He goes back to his work.)* After all, when God invented thieves he had to deprive them of a thing or two, so he took away from them the esteem of honest folk. When you come to think of it, it's not so terrible. It could have been much worse. *(He shrugs, and laughs, without daring to meet her eyes.)* In a little while, you'll see, we'll have forgotten all about it.

(He goes on collecting objects. She struggles again, and he looks at her.)

If there's anything you care for specially, you must tell me. I'll leave it for you, as a souvenir. I mean, I'd *like* to give you a little present.

(She looks at him and he stops in embarrassment.)

Please, don't look at me like that! You're breaking my heart! Can't you see I've got to do this? So just let me get quietly on with my job.

(She moves.)

Are you uncomfortable? You're not choking, are you? Look, Juliette, if you swear not to call out, I'll take the gag off. Do you swear?

(She nods.)

All right then, I trust you. *(He removes the handkerchief.)* What are you going to say to me, now that you know I'm a real thief? *(He sits down, resigned.)*

JULIETTE. *(The moment she is ungagged.)* This is absurd! Absolutely absurd! Untie me at once!

GUSTAVE. *Oh*, no! I'm a good sort, but business is business.

JULIETTE. At least listen to me!

GUSTAVE. What do you want to say?

JULIETTE. You don't imagine I came to find you, wearing my travelling coat, merely in order to sit here like a nincompoop bound and gagged in a chair? Of course I know you're a thief. If you weren't a real thief, I wouldn't have thought you were planning to leave in the middle of the night, would I, seeing you're a guest of my aunt's?

GUSTAVE. What are you talking about?

JULIETTE. I've been telling you over and over again for the last hour. I love you. I saw you take a car out of the garage, I guessed you really were a thief, and that tonight was the night. As I supposed you'd go the moment the job was done, I dressed and got ready to go with you. You don't intend to stay, do you?

GUSTAVE. That's no juestion to ask a thief.

JULIETTE. Well then, take me with you.

GUSTAVE. But I'm a thief.

JULIETTE. *(Crying out in exasperation)* I tell you I know you're a thief! There's no need to go on and on about it. I wonder you don't draw attention to yourself. Come along, untie my hands.

GUSTAVE. But, Juliette—

JULIETTE. Untie my hands. They're terribly painful.

GUSTAVE. Do you swear not to run away and raise the alarm?

JULIETTE. Yes, yes, I swear. Oh, how stupid you are!

GUSTAVE. I trust you of course, but I just don't understand.

(He unties her. She immediately powders her face, and then gets up with determination.)

JULIETTE. We've wasted at least a quarter of an hour. Make haste. It would do to get caught now. Have you enough with this lot? *(She indicates the sacks with her foot.)*

GUSTAVE. What are you doing?

JULIETTE. Really, I shall begin to wonder if you're all there soon. Yes, or no, do I appeal to you?

GUSTAVE. Oh yes, but—

JULIETTE. Good. That's the main thing. Now, listen to me. Gustave, if you like me, I love you and I want to be your wife—oh, don't worry, if you're afraid of awkward questions at the Registry Office, we won't get properly married. There. Now then— *(She picks up one of the sacks.)* Is this all we're taking with us?

GUSTAVE. *(Snatching the sack from her)* Juliette, no! You don't know what you're doing! You mustn't come with me. What would become of you?

JULIETTE. I'd help you. I'd keep a look-out, and I'd whistle when I saw someone coming. I can whistle beautifully. Listen— *(She gives an earsplitting whistle.)*

GUSTAVE. *(Terrified.)* Ssssh! For heaven's sake!

(They listen for a moment.)

JULIETTE. *(Humbly.)* I'm sorry. What a fool I am. Take me away. I'll whistle very quietly, I promise you, and then only when it's absolutely necessary.

GUSTAVE. Juliette, this is only a whim. You're playing with me. It's unkind of you.

JULIETTE. Oh no, you mustn't think that! Never think that! I love you.

GUSTAVE. But do you know the dangers of this kind of life?

JULIETTE. Yes. Kiss me.

GUSTAVE. Juliette, it's good-bye to your tranquallity.

JULIETTE. It was on the way to killing me, my tranquaillity. Kiss me.

GUSTAVE. But you're happy here, Juliette. You don't know what it means to be on the run, to be afraid. You're used to luxury.

JULIETTE. Why, we're rich! Look at this! If it worries you, we won't steal so long as the police are out looking for me.

GUSTAVE. Thieves aren't wealthy folk. You get precious little for what you sell.

JULIETTE. Well, we'll be poor then. Kiss me.

(They join in a long kiss.)

(Radiantly.) I am so happy. Now, hurry. *(She stops.)* Why, you haven't taken the little Fragonards. You're mad, my darling, they're the most valuable things in the house. *(She runs to take them down.)* And the little enamels. *(She rummages in the sack.)* Leave the candlesticks. They're imitation bronze. You see how useful I am to you. I shall be such a help, you'll see. Kiss me.

GUSTAVE. *(Taking her in his arms again)* My little robber girl.

(They go.)

ACT FOUR

In the conservatory, an hour later. The CLARINET, which has begun by playing the Carnival theme, takes it up again in a nostalgic manner. The CHARACTERS wander in in single file, heads hanging, and sit down, vexed and dejected.

LADY HURF. It's positively absurd.

HECTOR. I do think they might have let us in.

LADY HURF. Too absurd. Fancy writing the title of the Carnival in microscopic lettering. Economy is an absolute obsession with the French.

LORD EDGARD. We were turned away in the most humiliating fashion.

EVA. What do you expect, Uncle? I can quite see that our attire alarmed them.

LADY HURF. A Carnival of Leaves! The idiocy of it!! A Carnival of Leaves!

D.D. SENIOR. What puzzles me is how you could confuse a Carnival of Leaves with a Carnival of Thieves.

LADY HURF. You should have consulted the notices yourself then, my good friend, if your eyesight is so sharp.

D.D. SENIOR. But dammit—

D.D. JUNIOR. Don't be rash, Dad.

LADY HURF. To begin with, it's thanks to your disguises that our party was shown the door.

PETERBONO. I should definitely have got in, for one. It's a funny thing. They quite thought I was going as a palm tree.

LADY HURF. Of course, but for them we should all have been admitted. What abominable taste! Look at them, will you? They might be a couple of pantomime buccaneers.

D.D. SENIOR. I should have thought for a Carnival of Thieves—

LADY HURF. Leaves! Leaves! Leaves! Are you going to spend the rest of the evening calling it a Carnival of Thieves?

D.D. JUNIOR. Keep calm, Father. *(To* LADY HURF.)
We are dreadfully sorry.

D.D. SENIOR. *(Abjectly.)* We'll never do it again.

LADY HURF. A fine time to say so!

LORD EDGARD. Could we not perhaps spend the evening
as we are, among ourselves, so as not to waste our efforts
altogether?

LADY HURF. Edgard, what an insane idea. Let us go
up and change. We'll play yet one more stupefying game
of bridge.

(She sighs and the GUESTS *sigh with her.)*

LORD EDGARD. If I'd known we were going to play
bridge I would have preferred to keep my moustache.

LADY HURF. *(Distractedly.)* So would I! *(To* PETER-
BONO, *on her way out.)* My dear Duke, can you forgive
me for this wasted evening?

PETERBONO. *(Nudging* HECTOR) No evening is ever
really wasted.

LADY HURF. Another time I'll be more careful when I
read the posters, and more discriminating in my choice of
company.

(She goes with EVA *and* LORD EDGARD.)*

PETERBONO. Ring. Pearls.

HECTOR. Pocket-book.

PETERBONO. Perfect.

(The DUPONT-DUFORTS *find themselves alone.)*

D.D. SENIOR. Things are going badly.

D.D. JUNIOR. Very badly.

D.D. SENIOR. These gay dogs are here on the same
errand as we are, that's quite obvious, but everything is
going their way and nothing is coming ours.

D.D. JUNIOR. *(Looking in a mirror)* Yet we achieved a
really lovely make-up.

D.D. SENIOR. Not for a Carnival of Leaves.

D.D. JUNIOR. Fancy organising a Carnival of Leaves!

D.D. SENIOR. Fancy, what's more, reading "Carnival

of Thieves" when it's down in black and white on all the posters "Carnival of Leaves." The old goose!

D.D. JUNIOR. *(Catching sight of the drawing-room through the open window.)* Daddy!

D.D. SENIOR. What is it?

D.D. JUNIOR. Look at the wall!

D.D. SENIOR. What about the wall?

D.D. JUNIOR. The Fragonards!

D.D. SENIOR. If you think at a time like this I feel like going into ecstasies over a lot of paintings!

D.D. JUNIOR. Daddy, the Fragonards aren't on the wall. *(He rushes into the room.)*

D.D. SENIOR. Well?

D.D. JUNIOR. *(From the room.)* Nor are the enamels! The bronze candlesticks are missing! And the snuff-boxes. All the drawers are open! *(Rushing out again)* Daddy, there's been a burglary!

D.D. SENIOR. Let's go. They'll think we did it.

D.D. JUNIOR. Don't be ridiculous! We were at the carnival with everybody else! Daddy! There's been a robbery here!

D.D. SENIOR. *(Who has been to make sure.)* You're absolutely right. There's been a robbery. But what are you so pleased about? That won't set our affairs to rights.

D.D. JUNIOR. Don't you understand? There's been a robbery while we were at the Casino. Don't you see suspicion can only fall on the one person who made himself conspicuous by his absence? Now then, who, I ask you, made himself conspicuous by his absence?

D.D. SENIOR. Young Pedro?

D.D. JUNIOR. Of course! Young Pedro.

D.D. SENIOR. In that case, surely the others would be his accomplices.

D.D. JUNIOR. They are his accomplices. They came with us to allay suspicion, that's quite clear. But now you may be sure they're gone, or will have before very long.

D.D. SENIOR. Didier, you're magnificent! You do my old heart good. Kiss me, son! At last they are unmasked.

They're done for, laddie, and our affairs have never looked so promising.

D.D. JUNIOR. We must clinch matters. There's to be no escape and no denial. We must telephone the police at once. *(He picks up the receiver.)* Give me the police, please. And hurry!

D.D. SENIOR. *(Trundling round the drawing-room and bellowing)* The Fragonards! The enamels! The candlesticks! The snuff-boxes! Two drawers burst open! Magnificent!

D.D. JUNIOR. Hallo? Is that the police station? This is the Villa des Boyards. A serious robbery has just taken place. Yes, the thieves are still on the premises. You'll catch them red-handed if you hurry. Hurry!

D.D. SENIOR. *(Coming back radiant)* Come to your father, Laddie!

(They embrace.)

D.D. JUNIOR. Let's call the company and confront the rascals! Hey there! Come quickly, everybody!

D.D. SENIOR. Hey there! Hey!

LORD EDGARD. *(Entering. He, and likewise the OTHERS when they come down, have all changed back into their usual clothes.)* What's the matter?

D.D. JUNIOR. There's been a burglary!

LORD EDGARD. That's no surprise to anybody in these troubled times. Where?

D.D. JUNIOR. Here!

LORD EDGARD. Here!

D.D. SENIOR. *(Breathless with excitement.)* Here! Here in this very room!

LORD EDGARD. In the drawing-room? What did they take?

D.D. SENIOR. *(Like a street hawker.)* Fragonards! Enamels! Snuff-boxes! Candlesticks! Drawers! Come in and see! Come and see!

(LORD EDGARD goes into the room, comes back and staggers into an armchair.)

LORD EDGARD. Terrible! Terrible! I had an idea this would happen.

D.D. SENIOR.⎱ So had we!
D.D. JUNIOR.⎰

LORD EDGARD. Do you know who did it?

D.D. SENIOR. We have an idea!

LORD EDGARD. So have I!

(*Enter* EVA.)

My child, we've just been burgled!

EVA. What?

D.D. SENIOR. (*Off again.*) The Fragonards! The enamels! The candlesticks! The snuff-boxes!

EVA. I'm glad about the candlesticks, they were apalling. But it's a shame about the Fragonards.

HECTOR. (*Enters triumphantly in a new make-up.*) Eva, this time I've got it!

EVA. No.

LORD EDGARD. (*Leaping on him*) At last! The detective! My dear fellow, you're in the nick of time. A serious robbery has just been committed. We suspect some impostors whom we are entertaining at the moment, owing to a curious fancy of my cousin's. Kindly arrest them at once, my dear fellow.

EVA. What's come over you, Uncle? That's Prince Hector. Hector, do take off that beard.

HECTOR. (*Modestly, as he reveals himself.*) Yes sir, it's me.

LORD EDGARD. (*In a sudden rage.*) How much longer do you intend to make a fool of me, young man?

HECTOR. (*Backing imperceptibly towards the door*) But, your lordship, I'm not making a fool of you, really.

LORD EDGARD. I can take a joke, in doubtful taste though it is with a man of my years, but don't repeat it a dozen times a day!

HECTOR. (*Nearing the door*) But I'm not making a fool—

(*He bumps into the* DUPONT-DUFORTS, *who have cut off his retreat.*)

D.D. JUNIOR. Oh no.

D.D. SENIOR. Of course you're not making a fool of him. Don't go. Everything will be all right.

HECTOR. Look here, what's going on? Am I under suspicion?

EVA. Gentlemen, will you please leave His Highness alone?

HECTOR. I should think so. Why, it's absurd, isn't it, Eva?

LADY HURF. *(Entering with* PETERBONO*)* What is all this shouting? I've never heard such a commotion!

PETERBONO. We simply can't hear ourselves speak!

LORD EDGARD. It's terrible! There's been a dreadful robbery! I had my suspicions all along. I told you he died in 1904! I told you they were all impostors!

D.D. SENIOR. *(At the same time.)* The Fragonards! The enamels! The snuff-boxes! The candlesticks! The drawers!

LADY HURF. One at a time, please! I don't know what you're talking about. First of all I must sit down. I'm worn out.

(During the ejaculations of the OTHERS, *and the silence which follows,* HECTOR *is desperately indicating to* PETERBONO *that they must be off.* PETERBONO *thinks his cuff-links are undone, his tie crooked or that something is hanging down. He brushes himself, looks in the mirror, still fails to understand, and finally shrugs his shoulders and gives up.)*

LADY HURF. Now. Tell me all about it.

PETERBONO. *(Engagingly.)* Splendid idea. Tell us all about it.

LORD EDGARD. *(Before they stop him.)* Didn't I tell you he died in—

D.D. SENIOR. *(At the same time.)* Everything! Everything! The Fragonards! The—

(They look at each other and stop dead.)

EVA. There's been a burglary.

LADY HURF. A burglary?

EVA. Yes. While we were out the enamels were stolen, and the Fragonards, and believe it or not, the candlesticks.

LADY HURF. Oh good. They were imitation.

LORD EDGARD. I told you so! I told you so!

LADY HURF. One of the servants, I expect. Are they all here?

EVA. I don't know.

D.D. SENIOR. We must inform the police.

LADY HURF. No.

D.D. SENIOR. What do you mean, no?

LADY HURF. No, I tell you. I will not have policemen in my house.

D.D. JUNIOR. But we've already telephoned, your ladyship.

LADY HURF. My good sirs, have you completely forgotten your manners? I beg you to remember that this is my house. You appear to have abandoned every vestige of constraint these last few days.

D.D. JUNIOR. But we—

D.D. SENIOR. You see, we—

LADY HURF. Eva, ring through at once and tell them not to come.

D.D. SENIOR. Too late. They're bound to be on the way.

(*All this time* PETERBONO *and* HECTOR *have been quietly edging towards the door. When* LADY HURF *tells* EVA *to call off the police, they stop, still hopeful. At these last words, they make a frenzied dash for it.*)

Look! They're getting away!

D.D. JUNIOR. This is too much! We'll save you, whether you like it or not! Hands up!

D.D. SENIOR. Hands up!

(*They cover the* THIEVES *with their revolvers.*)

LADY HURF. Gentlemen, I am mistress in this house! I order you to put away those firearms!

D.D. JUNIOR. No!

D.D. SENIOR. No. You'll thank us for it later on.

LADY HURF. Eva, I'm going to have hysterics! Call the servants! Emile! Here, quickly! Joseph! Help!

(Enter POLICE, during her cries.)

POLICEMAN. Here we are! Horace, you take the fat one!

> *(They have seen these two horrible bandits pointing their guns at the gentry. Without a moment's indecision, they hurl themselves on the DUPONT-DUFORTS.)*

Aha, me beauties! We've got you!

D.D. SENIOR *and* JUNIOR. *(Backing away)* But—but— We didn't do anything! No, no, not us! Not us! Quite the reverse! We're the ones who telephoned! This is preposterous! It's they!

(They collide as they retreat, try to escape the other way and collide again, in the course of a droll little ballet which culminates in their capture.)

POLICEMEN. *(Hoisting them on to their shoulders with the showmanship of circus acrobats)* Upsadaisy! *(To HECTOR.)* If you'd like to give us a hand, sir, by taking the trouble to open the door, sir, it'd be much appreciated.

HECTOR. No trouble. Absolutely no trouble at all.

(The POLICEMEN carry off the DUPONT-DUFORTS despite their agonising protestations.)

LORD EDGARD. *(Wildly.)* But, my dear—

LADY HURF. *(Sternly.)* Edgard! Be quiet.

D.D. SENIOR. *(Yelling in vain as he is borne away)* For God's sake say something! Tell them! Tell them!

D.D. JUNIOR. *(As he whirls past her.)* Mademoiselle Eva!

(They have gone, played out by their own little melody.)

LADY HURF. *(Calmly.)* There! That's a relief. Three whole weeks those folk have been here, and I hadn't a notion how to get rid of them.

LORD EDGARD. *(Overcome by so many emotions, falls semi-conscious into an armchair.)* When I think I came here to cure my liver trouble!

LADY HURF. Eva dear, run up and get your uncle his smelling-salts.

> (EVA *goes.* LADY HURF *looks at* PETERBONO, *who ever since the arrest of the* DUPONT-DUFORTS *has been choking in the grip of irrepressible hysteria.)*

My dear man, save your laughter. I know perfectly well you are the real thief.

(He stops dead. She feels in his pocket.)

Give me back my pearls. You haven't been very clever.

PETERBONO. What do you mean?

LADY HURF. Have you a lot of luggage? How long will it take you to pack?

PETERBONO. *(Piteously.)* Not long.

LADY HURF. Then I advise you to make the greatest possible haste upstairs.

PETERBONO. Yes.

HECTOR. *(Enters. Superbly.)* There. The rascals are in good hands, your Ladyship.

(PETERBONO coughs.)

Father dear, are you not feeling well?

LADY HURF. No, he's not feeling at all well. I think you had better both go up to your rooms.

HECTOR. Really, Father? Where's the trouble exactly?

LORD EDGARD. *(Himself once more.)* I told you the Duke of Miraflores died in 1904!

LADY HURF. I knew it long ago, my dear.

HECTOR. *(Still not understanding* PETERBONO'S *desperate dumbshow, says waggishly:)* Ha! ha! ha! Still the same old joke, eh?

LADY HURF. The Duke died in my arms, or near enough. So that I knew quite well whom we were dealing with Only you see, my poor old Edgard, I was so very, very bored.

HECTOR. *(Finally going to* PETERBONO.) What's the matter, for heaven's sake?

PETERBONO. Idiot! I've been trying to tell you for the

last half-hour. The game's up, but she's letting us go
free.

HECTOR. Uh? Don't be silly, they've arrested the others.

LADY HURF. *(Going to them with a smile)* You don't,
I'm sure, want to await the visit of the inspector of police,
gentlemen.

HECTOR. This is unthinkable! What are we accused of?
We were with you the whole evening!

PETERBONO. Don't be canny. Come on.

HECTOR. My dear father, I don't know what you're
talking about. Madam, we are here as your guests, and
this robbery is no reason to treat us, the Miraflores y
Grandes, in this cavalier fashion.

PETERBONO. *(Unable to suppress a giggle, despite the
tragic situation.)* Miraflores y Grandes! Oh, my Lord!
You're off your head, old chap. Come on.

LADY HURF. Go along, sir, do, as everyone advises you.

HECTOR. I will not tolerate this attitude. *(To* PETER-
BONO.) Play up, will you?

EVA. *(Coming back)* Here are the salts.

HECTOR. I will not tolerate this attitude. Because if
you consider our presence undesirable, I laugh to scorn—
do you hear, to scorn, your utterly unfounded and insult-
ing allegations. There's someone here, I know, who will
think my presence far from undesirable. Eva, Eva my
darling, I've found my face at last! *(He turns away and
rapidly recreates the appearance he had in the first scene.)*

PETERBONO. Hector, stop playing about. The police are
on their way.

HECTOR. *(Making up.)* Let me alone. We're saved, I
tell you!

LADY HURF. *(Sits down, dispirited.)* Edgard, if this
headstrong child falls in love with him again, the situation is absolutely hopeless.

LORD EDGARD. I have not the faintest idea of what is
going on. What is he doing? Is this another piece of
comicality? He goes very much too far, that boy.

HECTOR. *(Turning round triumphantly.)* Eva beloved!
It *was* like this, wasn't it?

(A silence. Eva looks at him. The Others hold their breath.)

EVA. *(Calmly breaking the tension)* Yes, that's how you were. Only I must have looked at you too hastily, I think, because now you don't appeal to me at all.

LADY HURF. *(Leaping up)* Heaven be praised! Now, off with you! Quickly, off with you!

HECTOR. But, Eva, listen! Eva, I can't believe—

PETERBONO. *(In a whisper.)* Hurry, idiot, hurry! She's taken back the necklace, but I've still got the ring.

(They go with great dignity. A gay little TUNE signals their departure.)

LADY HURF. *(Watching them go with a tender little smile)* Poor old fellow. I let him keep the ring. They stayed here a full fortnight after all, because of me. We haven't any right to make them waste their time. I imagine it's a trade which can't bring in all that much.

LORD EDGARD. What I don't fathom is where the boy comes in.

(The TWO WOMEN look at him in sudden anguish.) The boy, the young one, who was so pleasant, you remember?

EVA. Juliette! Where's Juliette?

LADY HURF. Juliette! She didn't come to the Carnival Isn't she upstairs? Perhaps in the morning-room? Or in the garden?

EVA. I'll run and see. Oh, it's inconceivable.

LORD EDGARD. What is inconceivable? I don't understand, quite.

(LADY HURF drops on to the sofa, and plays nervously with her pearls.) Why do you look so tragic? It's all over now, isn't it?

LADY HURF. No, stupid, it is not all over. This boy has carried off Juliette along with the pictures in the drawing-room. How many times did I tell you to bestir yourself and take precautions if we didn't want disaster?

EVA. *(Coming back)* She's not upstairs. The servants are combing the grounds.

LADY HURF. It's horrible!

LORD EDGARD. Juliette, our little Juliette. Is it possible? Can she have been stolen?

EVA. Yes.

LORD EDGARD. But she's a big girl now. She could have defended herself. Or called for help. The house is overrun with staff.

LADY HURF. Can't you understand? She's in his power! He's bewitched her. He'll make her steal for him, or walk the streets!

LORD EDGARD. The streets. *(It dawns on him.)* The streets! *(He staggers under the blow.)*

(The CLARINET plays an air heavy with tragedy. The three of them lapse into pensive and painful silence. The CLARINET resumes its tragic theme with an overtone of mockery, and then leads into the romance which is indeed altogether fitting at this moment, for GUSTAVE enters on tiptoe, laden with so many things that he cannot see where he is going. He is carrying JULIETTE, who is asleep, and his various sacks. He crosses the drawing-room, unseen by anybody; suddenly he bumps into an armchair. He drops his sacks with a clatter, and startles the OTH-ERS, who see him and cry out.)

He's killed her!

(GUSTAVE, terrified, makes to put JULIETTE down on the sofa, but at the cries she wakens and clings to him.)

JULIETTE. No, no, no! Why did you bring me back? No, he's not to go! If he goes I'm going with him!

LADY HURF. Juliette!

LORD EDGARD. My child.

JULIETTE. *(Screaming through a flood of tears)* Yes, you despise him, I know, but I love him. Don't try to tell me anything—I want to go with him because I love him. Don't say a word, I'd only hate you for it. Gustave, Gustave, why did you bring me back?

(He struggles and tries to run away but she clutches him.)

No. Stay here, or let me come with you. Why did you bring me back? Was I too stupid for you? To naïve? Is it because I fell asleep beside you in the car that you don't want me? It's true one doesn't as a rule doze off the night of one's elopement, but I was tired, my darling. I'm not used to staying up so late. *(She hides her head in his arms.)*

LORD EDGARD. What is she saying?

LADY HURF. *(Moved.)* Do be quiet! It's very lovely what she is saying.

JULIETTE. *(Turning to them like a little fury, without letting go of* GUSTAVE*)* No, no, I'm not ashamed! I'm not ashamed! You can say anything you like, I'll never be ashamed! I love him. I want him for my lover, since you will never let him be my husband. Look. I'm going to kiss him now in front of you.

(She throws her arms round his neck. He holds back for a second, then as he sees her tousled hair and her radiant tear-stained face, he too forgets the OTHERS*.)*

GUSTAVE. I love you, Juliette.

JULIETTE. You see, we're kissing here, in front of them.

(They kiss.)

LORD EDGARD. *(Adjusting his pince-nez)* Why, they're kissing.

LADY HURF. That's right. They're kissing. What about it? Did you never do as much? *(She contemplates them, entranced.)* How enchanting they are!

LORD EDGARD. Aren't they? Do you remember, Emily?

LADY HURF. They make a delightful couple, don't they?

LORD EDGARD. *(Lost in his memories.)* Delightful. Do you remember? The Crystal Palace?

LADY HURF. She's nearly as tall as he is. He is adorable. Look at the breeding in that profile. The exquisite shyness and yet the strength of it. He will make a fairy-tale hus-

band for our terrible, gentle little Juliette. *(She stops.)*
Edgard, what are you talking me into? He's a thief!

LORD EDGARD. *(Smiling)* Ah yes, a thief.

LADY HURF. Well then, it's out of the question. He must
go at once.

(The CLARINET stops from shock.)

LORD EDGARD. *(Crestfallen.)* But—but they love each
other.

LADY HURF. I know they love each other. But it's the
only thing to do. Absolutely the only thing. She simply
cannot marry a boy who has neither a father nor a mother.

LORD EDGARD. Ah! *(He thinks furiously for a moment,
then cries suddenly.)* Wait a minute! Wait a minute!

*(GUSTAVE and JULIETTE, startled by his cry, come out of
their embrace. LORD EDGARD runs out like one de-
mented.)*

LADY HURF. Where do you suppose he's going?

JULIETTE. I'll never leave him, never, never, never.

GUSTAVE. *(Holding her to him, says by way of ex-
planation)* We love each other.

(The CLARINET plays a little supplication.)

LADY HURF. I gather so. But there it is. You're nothing
but a nobody, if not worse. I'm afraid you'll have to go.

(Another entreaty from the CLARINET.)

JULIETTE. If he goes I go with him.

LADY HURF. This time we will be here to stop you.

*(The CLARINET screams in heart-rending implora-
tion. LADY HURF turns furiously on the MUSICIAN.)*
As for you, my good sir, you're beginning to get on my
nerves! Go away!

(The CLARINET attempts a musical protest.)
Get out of here this instant!

*(She drives him out. Pathetically the MUSICIAN goes,
expressing his despair on his instrument. LORD ED-*

GARD *returns like a meteor carrying ribbons, medals and a photograph. He marches threateningly over to* GUSTAVE.)

LORD EDGARD. You are twenty years old, are you not?
GUSTAVE. Yes.
LORD EDGARD. Right. *(He looks at the photograph, looks at it a second time, backs, screwing up his eyes in the manner of a painter scrutinizing a picture.)* Hold your head up. Fine. Open your shirt. Fine. Now for the mark behind the ear. *(He turns back his ear.)* Fine. *(He shows him the medal.)* Do you recognize this medal?
GUSTAVF. No.
LORD EDGARD. *(Throwing it away)* Never mind. You are my son! My son who was stolen from me at a tender age. *(He falls into his arms.)*
LADY HURF. Edgard, have you taken leave of your senses?
GUSTAVE. *(Furiously)* Let me go, sir. I don't know what you're talking about. *(To* JULIETTE.) What's the matter with him?
LORD EDGARD. *(To* LADY HURF.) Do you deny that a son was stolen from me at a tender age? *(To* GUSTAVE.) Do you deny that you are uncertain of your paternal origins? Yes, yes, you are my son, my own son, my beloved son! *(He falls on his neck again.)*
JULIETTE. Isn't that lucky! Gustave, isn't that lucky!
GUSTAVE. *(Freeing himself roughly)* No, it won't work.
LORD EDGARD. What won't work?
GUSTAVE. I'm quite sure I'm not your son.
LORD EDGARD. So I shall have waited twenty years for Heaven to give me back my child, and now when Heaven at last sees fit to give him back to me, it is this very child who refuses to acknowledge his own father!
GUSTAVE. No. It's all a scheme because you can see your little girl is in love with me, but I'm sorry, I can't accept.
LADY HURF. That's very honourable of him.

LORD EDGARD. This is horrible! Horrible! My son denies me! *(He prances with rage.)*

GUSTAVE. No, I can't accept. It's nice of you to do it, very nice of you. But I can't. I'm not one of your sort.

LADY HURF. It is really unfortunate that this boy should be the only one amongst us to suffer from class-consciousness.

LORD EDGARD. I am abominably humiliated. Such contempt from my own son! I shall crumple up with sorrow. *(He does in fact crumple up with sorrow on the nearest sofa.)* Here I am, crumpled up. How much longer do I have to stay crumpled?

LADY HURF. Couldn't you see your way to accepting? You're making your father very unhappy.

GUSTAVE. How can I! I haven't any reason—

JULIETTE. Oh, but you have! Come into the garden as you did before. I'm going to explain all your reasons to you. Do come, please. Come anyway. You haven't anything to lose after all, by coming into the garden.

(She drags him out.)

LADY HURF. *(As soon as they're gone.)* Edgard, it's not true! You never had a son stolen from you at a tender age!

LORD EDGARD. No, it isn't true. It's a picture I cut out of a magazine.

LADY HURF. So you've acted like an imbecile for over fifty years and yet you had it in you to think of that all by yourself.

EVA. How happy they are going to be.

LADY HURF. *(Dreamily.)* Yes.

EVA. And I shall continue to play the young and charming widow who is always such a great success.

LADY HURF. My poor Eva, faith is a gift, alas, and there's no learning it. It's over, our fine escapade. Here we are alone again, like bobbing corks. It's only for those who have played it with all the zest of youth that the comedy is a success, and only then because they were playing their youth, a thing which succeeds always. They were not even conscious of the comedy.

(Enter a BEARDED GENTLEMAN.*)*

BEARDED GENTLEMAN. I am from Scotland Yard.

LORD EDGARD. *(Lets out a roar, leaps onto him and pulls his beard.)* Oh no, it won't work this time!

DETECTIVE. Stop it! You're hurting me!

LORD EDGARD. *(Greatly astonished.)* What! Do you mean it's your own?

DETECTIVE. Of course it's my own!

LORD EDGARD. Then you really are the detective I sent for?

DETECTIVE. I've just said so, haven't I?

LORD EDGARD. Well we don't need you any more. The entertainment is over.

DETECTIVE. *(Blithely.)* In that case—

(He pulls his clarinet out of his pocket—for it is none other than the MUSICIAN—*and strikes up a quick-step which does duty as a finale. The* CHARACTERS *come in through all the doors, dancing and exchanging beards.)*

THE END

FAVORITE
BROADWAY COMEDIES
from
SAMUEL FRENCH, INC.

BAREFOOT IN THE PARK – BEDROOM FARCE –
BLITHE SPIRIT – BUTTERFLIES ARE FREE –
CALIFORNIA SUITE – CHAMPAGNE COMPLEX –
CHAPTER TWO – COME BLOW YOUR HORN – DA –
THE GINGERBREAD LADY – GOD'S FAVORITE –
THE GOOD DOCTOR – HAPPY BIRTHDAY,
WANDA JUNE – HAY FEVER – HOW THE OTHER
HALF LOVES – I OUGHT TO BE IN PICTURES –
JUMPERS – KNOCK KNOCK – LAST OF THE RED
HOT LOVERS – MY FAT FRIEND – NEVER TOO LATE
– NIGHT AND DAY – THE NORMAN CONQUESTS –
NORMAN, IS THAT YOU? – THE ODD COUPLE –
OTHERWISE ENGAGED – THE OWL AND THE
PUSSYCAT – THE PRISONER OF 2ND AVENUE –
THE PRIVATE EAR AND THE PUBLIC EYE –
THE RAINMAKER – SAME TIME, NEXT YEAR –
THE SHOW OFF – 6 RMS RIV VU – THE SUNSHINE
BOYS – A THOUSAND CLOWNS – TRAVESTIES –
TWIGS – TWO FOR THE SEASAW

*For descriptions of these and all our plays, consult our Basic
Catalogue of Plays.*

TALKING WITH . . .
(LITTLE THEATRE)
By JANE MARTIN

11 women—Bare stage

Here, at last, is the collection of eleven extraordinary monologues for eleven actresses which had them on their feet cheering at the famed Actors Theatre of Louisville—audiences, critics and, yes, even jaded theatre professionals. The mysteriously pseudonymous Jane Martin is truly a ''find'', a new writer with a wonderfully idiosyncratic style, whose characters alternately amuse, move and frighten us always, however, speaking to us from the depths of their souls. The characters include a baton twirler who has found God through twirling; a fundamentalist snake handler, an ex-rodeo rider crowded out of the life she has cherished by men in 3-piece suits who want her to dress up ''like Minnie damn Mouse in a tutu''; an actress willing to go to any length to get a job; and an old woman who claims she once saw a man with ''cerebral walrus'' walk into a McDonald's and be healed by a Big Mac. ''Eleven female monologues, of which half a dozen verge on brilliance.''—London Guardian. ''Whoever (Jane Martin) is, she's a writer with an original imagination.''—Village Voice. ''With Jane Martin, the monologue has taken on a new poetic form, intensive in its method and revelatory in its impact.''—Philadelphia Inquirer. ''A dramatist with an original voice . . . (these are) tales about enthusiasms that become obsessions, eccentric confessionals that levitate with religious symbolism and gladsome humor.''—N.Y. Times. *Talking With . . .* is the 1982 winner of the American Theatre Critics Association Award for Best Regional Play. (#22009)

(Royalty, $60–$40.
If individual monologues are done separately: Royalty, $15–$10.)

HAROLD AND MAUDE
(ADVANCED GROUPS—COMEDY)
By COLIN HIGGINS

9 men, 8 women—Various settings

Yes: *the Harold and Maude!* This is a stage adaptation of the wonderful movie about the suicidal 19 year-old boy who finally learns how to truly *live* when he meets up with that delightfully whacky octogenarian, Maude. Harold is the proverbial Poor Little Rich Kid. His alienation has caused him to attempt suicide several times, though these attempts are more cries for attention than actual attempts. His peculiar attachment to Maude, whom he meets at a funeral (a mutual passion), is what saves him—and what captivates us. This new stage version, a hit in France directed by the internationally-renowned Jean-Louis Barrault, will certainly delight both afficionados of the film and new-comers to the story. ''Offbeat upbeat comedy.''—Christian Science Monitor. (#10032)

(Royalty, $60–$40.)
